This

here 'cos a

book looks

incomplete

without a

blank page at

the front of it

Published by:
Moonbeams Publishing
20 Hambleton Terrace
York
YO31 8JJ

CONTENTS

THE NATURE OF HAPPINESS

Eternity

He who binds himself to the
wings of joy
Does the winged life destroy;
But he who kisses the joy as
it flies
Lives in eternity's sunrise.

William Blake (1757-1827)

Not having some of what
you want is an integral
part of being happy

Man wishes to be happy
even when he so lives
as to make happiness
impossible - St Augustine
(354-430)

Happiness is like a
sunbeam, which the least
shadow intercepts
- Chinese Proverb

Love
Is
Not
All
You
Need
But
It
Helps
A
Lot

The happy man
is not he who
seems thus to
others, but
who seems
thus to himself
- Pubilius Syrus
(1st Cent BC)

In the world
        there are
                only two
                        tragedies.

                        One is
                not getting
            what one
    wants, and
            the other
                    is getting it

- Oscar Wilde (1854-1900)

Happiness is not the absence of misery. Absence of misery by itself leads to a state of non-being. It is maintained by escapism - such as burying oneself in work and hedonism. Happiness is true elation, a state of mind which cannot be mistaken.

Remember those times of happiness for, at times, they can keep you going like oases in a desert.

Happiness cannot be sought directly - it is a cause of something else.

It is neither wealth nor splendour, but tranquillity and occupation, which give happiness - Thomas Jefferson (1743-1826)

There are many roads to happiness if the gods assent - Pindar (518-438 BC)

No man is happy who does not think himself so - Pubilius Syrus (1st Cent BC)

There is nothing good or bad, but thinking makes it so - Shakespeare (1564-1616)

True happiness is of a retired nature, and an enemy to pomp and noise; it arises, in the first place, from the enjoyment of one's self, and, in the next, from the friendship and conversation of a few select companions - Joseph Addison (1672-1719)

IMPORTANCE
OF HAPPINESS

There is no duty we under-rate as the
duty of being happy
- Robert Louis Stevenson (1850-1894)

Man... has never learned that the sole
purpose of life is to enjoy it
- Samuel Butler (1835-1902)

One moment may with bliss repay
unnumbered hours of pain
- Thomas Campbell (1777-1844)

We should consider every day lost on
which we have not danced at least once
- Nietzsche (1844-1900)

BALANCE

Remember the unhappy times and learn from them, for happiness and unhappiness are like hardness and softness - you would have no concept of one unless you'd experienced both.

Learn from the past, plan for the future, party for today.

All of man's unhappiness derives from one simple thing: his inability to sit alone in a room - Pascal (1623-1662)

Although a certain amount of introspection is necessary, and this amount varies from individual to individual, an overindulgence becomes nothing more than self-indulgence. There is nothing romantic about the self-inflicted agonies of someone who could avoid them if they so chose to by going out in the world and exploring its many challenges, joys and pitfalls, thus allowing themselves to grow instead of stagnating in the rut they have thought themselves into.

HARMONY

To get wound up by circumstance is to destroy the moment - destroy your own happiness. Rejoice in small inconveniences for it is by seeing these through with serenity that makes you a better person.

> Appreciate, learn from and work with
> whatever happens in everyday life.
> The natural result of this harmonious
> way of living is happiness.

Enjoy the simple and the quiet,
the natural and the plain.
Do not think about things too much,
but do them spontaneously.
This will bring happiness.
Alas, our society regards a person who
follows these principles as a naive fool.

What is so wonderful about fresh snow, clean air and pure water?

Nothing...

absolutely Nothing.

<u>SOME SYMPTOMS OF</u>
<u>INNER PEACE</u>

- A tendency to think and act spontaneously rather than on fears based on past experiences
- An unmistakable ability to enjoy each moment
- A loss of interest in judging other people
- A loss of interest in interpreting the actions of other people
- A loss of interest in conflict
- A loss of ability to worry
- Frequent, overwhelming episodes of appreciation
- Contented feelings of connectedness with nature and others
- Frequent attacks of smiling
- An increasing tendency to let things happen rather than make them happen
- An increased susceptibility to the love extended by others as well the uncontrollable urge to love them back.

Author Unknown

CHAOS

Life is frequently chaotic. We can try to control this chaos so we can get more out of life, but in our attempts to do so, we forget to enjoy life. Sometimes it is better to go along with the chaos. Often, controlling it will only bring the unhappiness we wish to banish. Instead, it is better to use chaos to have fun and adventure. After all, what is more interesting, a journey where you know the scenery, or a journey where everything is new and fresh?

TIME

If you find yourself with unexpected time on your hands because of a delayed train or an appointment unexpectedly cancelled or any other reason, rejoice and use that time wisely. You could read a book or a newspaper, plan your next day, take a much needed nap or do whatever you like!

Try not to live as if time were a reality which can steal your life away.

<u>STRENGTH</u>

It's
a
good
life
if
you
don't
weaken.

HEDONISM

Much of the our society tries to derive happiness from excesses. Eating too much, drinking too much, working too much and exercising too much are the more common ones. Our society seems to compartmentalise everything. Including happiness. But, unfortunately, this way of trying to be happy often leads to the exact opposite.

KEEPING HAPPY FROM MOMENT TO MOMENT

Keeping happy from moment to moment is a way of life which is only sometimes under-rated because mostly it is totally ignored!

Occasionally stop and ask what you like about yourself and what things have gone well recently.

If you look at your memories, you hone in on specific moments. The event you think about may have stretched over days, weeks or years, but your memories of it will be specific moments. We all live moment to moment. Create and collect as many joyful, special moments as you can and, if ever you're feeling down or find yourself thinking about some unpleasant incident from the past, recall one of these moments. You will find your spirits immediately lifting.

Human felicity is produced not so much by great pieces of good fortune that seldom happen as by little advantages that occur every day - Benjamin Franklin (1706-1790)

Look to this day
For yesterday is but a
dream
And tomorrow is only
a vision
But today, well lived,
Makes every yester-
day a dream of happiness
And every tomorrow a
vision of hope
Look well, therefore,
to this day
Sanskrit Proverb

SELF-KNOWLEDGE

There is no one meaning to all lives. Each person must look to themselves to teach themselves the meaning of their lives. It is only through self-knowledge (which is gained through experiencing different things and reflecting) that one can even begin to try to follow the path which will give them the greatest satisfaction.

Many people are stuck in the wrong job, the wrong marriage, or the wrong house. When you know and respect your own inner nature, you know where you belong. You also know where you don't belong. One person's food is often another person's poison, and what is glamorous and exciting to some can be a dangerous trap to others.

21

Half
the battle
of fulfilling ones
needs is knowing
what they
are!

Happiness is in the taste, and not in
the things; we are happy from
possessing what we like, not from
possessing what others like
- La Rochefoucauld (1613-1680)

When you discover something you don't like about yourself you can ignore it, eradicate it, change it into something else or find a beneficial use for it. If you are going to ignore it, not only will you be left with the problem, but you will be snubbing a potentially valuable insight. To eradicate it will take a lot of effort and will probably be the least successful path - after all, it takes more energy to stop a force dead in its tracks than to divert it. To find a beneficial use for it or change it into something else is like using flooded land to grow rice rather than moving to another area only to find you have a different set of problems there which you are less well equipped to deal with. Remember: the bad can be the raw material for the good.

You may find that the way to happiness in your life is to change nothing, except yourself. And, although people often say: "That's just the way I am - I can't change." This is self-defeating. We can all change the way we are to some extent.

If you truly know yourself, others opinions are meaningless.

Ask yourself what you are running from, and to, and why.

Learn what you are and be such - Pindar (518-438 BC)

<u>SELF-ESTEEM</u>

The approval of others is pleasant but not essential. In order to live life fully we need to express ourselves, which means that at times we will do things of which others disapprove. If we are constantly trying to avoid disapproval we will either become passive individuals or people with a poor sense of self.

A man cannot be comfortable without his
own approval
- Mark Twain (1835-1910)

For the sake of your self esteem and mental health forgive yourself. And again. And again. And again. And again. And again...

Self-
love, my
liege, is
not so
vile a
sin as
self-
neglect-
ing.

-

Shakes
peare
(1564-
1616)

LUCK

Reporter: "You were pretty lucky with that last shot, weren't you?"

Golfer: "You know, it's funny: the more I practice the luckier I get."

Luck occurs when preparation meets opportunity.

MONEY

The conviction of the rich that the poor are happy is no more foolish than the conviction of the poor that the rich are - Mark Twain (1835-1910)

It is good to have money and the things money can buy but it is wise to occasionally check that, in its pursuit, you haven't lost the things that it can't buy.

"Money won't bring happiness" - the earning and possession of money has brought a lot more happiness than has poverty.

The possession of gold has ruined fewer men than the lack of it. What noble enterprises have been checked and what fine souls have been blighted in the gloom of poverty the world will never know - Thomas Bailey Aldrich (1836-1907)

Resolve not to be poor: whatever you have spend less. Poverty is a great enemy of human happiness; it certainly destroys liberty, and it makes some virtues impracticable and others extremely difficult - Samuel Johnson (1709-1784)

Poverty with joy is not poverty at all. The poor man is not one who has little, but one who hankers after more - Seneca (4BC-AD65)

It is said that the average American family are three pay cheques away from homelessness. Living within your means isn't extending your income to the maximum number of HP agreements and the best food you can afford and nights out as often as possible. Put some away for a rainy day and sleep a little easier knowing you won't get wet should the rain come.

In our society, money is often looked upon as the central focus of existence. Taking an interest in the finer things in life is regarded as foolish or besides the point.

Personal development and money run hand in hand: the higher you rise in your profession the bigger your pay cheque.

Money and respect are synonymous. Money seems to have a mystical element about it: the ones who don't have it hold the ones who do have it in awe.

The quality of justice depends on the money behind you.

With money one has freedom. The freedom to take a holiday or buy a better car. With money one has security. One's old age provided for and the best health care ensured. However, in time these luxuries become necessities. As you climb higher on the ladder of the rat race, you moves into richer social circles. If a person falls to a lower level, they will lose all their "friends", as they will become undesirable in the strata which leave them behind. They will also become undesirable in the strata they enter because they don't belong in that class. The public school fees and Harley Street clinics are no longer luxuries for the people who use them - they are an essential reflection of social standing. It is terrifying to imagine life without them. You don't own money, it owns you.

Money gives freedom. Those who don't have enough to feed themselves or their families are easily manipulated and enslaved by the rich. The poor countries are treated in the same way by the rich countries. Either be poor and be the manipulated, or be rich and be the manipulator for the price of having money as one's master. The later role is by far the more desirable, but both steal that most fundamental of things from one - human dignity.

Money is proof of not having lived in vain. But the designer lifestyle means strip mining, carbon monoxide and acid rain. But how can this be avoided? There are so many essentials which you have to have to survive in this society - a house, a car, hot water, central heating, double glazing, a stereo, a TV, a telephone, redecorating and replacing furniture at least every ten years, disposable nappies, keeping up with the latest fads, home improvement, luxury foods, expensive bars and restaurants, designer clothes... The only real choice is fulfilment through consumerism. If you seek fulfilment through any other means you will be outcast. Charity work is no option - you are thought of as no more than some sort of do-gooder, trying to increase your standing in society and/or relieve a half-guilty conscience. You are not allowed to feel the fulfilment of a "self made man". If you want anything through any medium other than money you have to fight society tooth and nail all the way, and face the fact that you'll probably lose, just like everyone else who tried - at best they are looked upon as some historical anomaly to be respected but not taken too seriously.

Greed is infectious. It is a disease nobody can resist, especially when bombarded so ruthlessly.

POWER

To know the pains of power, we must go to those who have it; to know its pleasures, we must go to those seeking it - Charles Caleb Colton (1780-1832)

RELATING TO OTHERS

No man can be happy without a friend, nor be sure of his friend until he is unhappy - Thomas Fuller (1608-1661)

More faults are often committed while we are trying to oblige than while we are giving offence – Tacitus (56-117)

If youth is wasted on the young, old age is wasted on the elderly. All they ever seem to use their accumulated wisdom, knowledge and experience for is to complain about the young.

It takes a brave person to admit they were wrong and apologise. It takes an arrogant fool not to.

When you are young you will do foolish things. You will be aggressive when trying to be assertive and over-timid when trying to be reasonable. When it comes to talking to people you fancy, you will make an unbelievable fool of yourself... Just like all the generations before you and all the ones to follow. In a couple of years you will look back and think "How could I have been so stupid". In a further couple of years you will realise it was all part of your learning experience.

You <u>will</u> do foolish things, but when you do, don't take it too seriously. Pick yourself up, dust yourself off and get ready for the next time you embarrass yourself. The more often you do it, the quicker it's out of the way.

We all make mistakes. If you do not forgive others for the ones they make you will soon find yourself with no friends.

Everyone has shortcomings. You will never find that perfect person, that one person for you. The question you must ask yourself, in your opinion, does a person's positive attributes outweigh their shortcomings? If they do, it could be the beginning of a friendship.

You will find that the attitude with which you approach the world will be returned to you. If you approach it with a smile and kindness you will get the same back. That is not to say that you will necessarily get it back from the people who you treat with respect - you may get the opposite - but generally you will. You will also be more receptive when it happens. If you approach the world with cynicism, bitterness and misery, people will more often than not react to you in the same way, and when kindness is shown to you you will rarely notice it.

People need other people, but to rely on others for your self-esteem diminishes your own personal sense of power.

He who fears you present will hate you absent -
Thomas Fuller (1608-1661)

Do not worry about the friends who no longer contact you or take an interest in you - concentrate on the ones who do.

The first thing to learn in intercourse with others is non-interference with their own particular ways of being happy, provided those ways do not assume to interfere by violence with others - William James (1842-1910)

The opinions which we hold of one another, our relations with friends and kinsfolk are in no sense permanent, save in appearance, but are as eternally fluid as the sea itself - Marcel Proust (1871-1922)

Those faults you find most intolerable in others are generally the ones you find most intolerable in yourself.

<u>IMPORTANCE OF FRIENDSHIP</u>

We do not so much need the help of our friends as the confidence of their help in need - Epicurus (342-270 BC)

A good friend is my nearest relation
- Thomas Fuller (1608-1661)

Have friends. 'Tis a second existence
- Baltasar Gracian (1809-1894)

Although, at worst, self destructive and, at best, morally lamentable, it cannot be denied that one uses one's early friends as a marker against which to judge one's progress through life.

Friends are often used as (mostly) non-physical punchbags upon which to take out the frustrations caused by life.

Life is partly what we make it, and partly what it is made by the friends we choose.

Sharing good times with another doubles that joy. Sharing woes with another halves that unhappiness.

NATURE OF
FRIENDSHIP

Without wearing any mask we are conscious of,
we have a special face for each friend
- Oliver Wendell Holmes (1809-1894)

A new friend is like a new wine; when it has
aged you will drink with pleasure - Apocrypha

Wishing to be friends is quick work, but
friendship is a slow-ripening fruit
– Aristotle (384-322 BC)

Friendship is a strong and habitual
inclination in two persons to promote
the good and happiness of one another
- Eustace Budgell (1686-1737)

There is nothing quite like making friends with
someone who you once despised.

True friendship is like sound health; the value
of it is seldom known until it is lost
- Charles Caleb Colton (1780-1832)

The only way to have a friend is to be one -
Emerson (1803-1882)

Real friendship is shown in times of trouble;
prosperity is full of friends
- Euripides (485-406 BC)

Make an effort to acquaint yourself with every
decent person you meet. In time some will fall
by the wayside, but others will become friends.

Friendship, like credit, is highest where it is
not used - Elbert Hubbard (1859-1915)

That a friendship may at once be fond and
lasting, there must not only be equal virtue on
each part, but virtue of the same kind; not only
the same end must be proposed, but the same
means must be approved by both - Samuel
Johnson (1709-1784)

When my friends are one-eyed,
I look at them in profile
- Joseph Joubert (1754-1824)

With time, many friendships cease to be such. The fact is that people grow apart. When this happens it is best to let them go. To try to maintain a defunct friendship is painful on both sides.

What we commonly call friendships are nothing but acquaintance and familiarities, either occasionally contracted or upon some design, by means of which there happens some little intercourse between our souls - Montaigne (1533-1592)

Very few friendships are made up of two minds which think exactly alike. Friends are nearly always such in parts.

Spontaneous friendships are formed on the
instinct of two people. They manage to form
a bond, knowing that they see eye to eye on
many things by observation of a few. But be
warned - such instinct can be misleading.
Any friendship takes time to mature.

> One who's our friend is fond of us; one
> who's fond of us isn't necessarily our
> friend - Seneca (4BC-AD65)

To throw away an honest friend is to throw
your life away - Sophocles (496-406 BC)

> How often we find ourselves turning our
> backs on our actual Friends, that we may go
> and meet their ideal cousins
> - Thoreau (1817-1862)

Friendship is the marriage of the soul,
and this marriage is liable to divorce
- Voltaire (1694-1778)

WORK

A great deal of current unhappiness comes from having the time to consider whether one is happy or unhappy.

Work as if you will live forever: live as if you will die tomorrow

<u>STRESS</u>

The surest way of failing is by trying too hard.

When you are next busy, rushing around trying to get something done, ask yourself why are you doing it? What will you gain? Is it worth putting yourself through all the stress that you are? If the answer is no, stop doing it. If the answer is yes, is there any way you can do it but enjoy what you are doing by changing your attitude towards it? Can you laugh more, take a more relaxed attitude, but still get it done in time? By being more relaxed, will this necessarily slow you down? You will find that, by taking this approach, you may get it done quicker and you will definitely be happier. And what else is life about? It's certainly too short to take so seriously.

<u>WORRY & PROBLEMS</u>

<u>Princess Ida</u>

Oh, don't the days seem lank and long,
When all goes right and nothing goes
wrong
And isn't your life extremely flat
With nothing whatever to grumble at!
- W S Gilbert (1836-1911)

My life has been full of
terrible misfortunes...
most of which never
happened - Montaigne
(1533-1592)

Worry is often a sustained form of fear caused by indecision.

Prudence keeps life safe,
but does not often make it happy
- Samuel Johnson (1709-1784)

Jealousy and anger shorten life, and anxiety brings on old age too soon -
Apocrypha

As a rule, what is out of sight disturbs men's minds more seriously than what they see - Julius Caesar (100-44 BC)

If something which appears disastrous happens, ask yourself if it will matter in one year. This will put it into perspective.

The difference between happy and unhappy people is not lack of problems, but determination to solve them. This requires considered thought and then acting upon that thought. The last thing you should do is what a great many people seem to do: ask advice from people even less qualified than they are about the situation and, even then, ignore that advice.

If you are worried, talk to someone you trust. How often is it that you have found that you have blown something out of all proportion when you have mulled over it by yourself? Talking it over with others often helps to put it into perspective.

John Paul Getty used to say that before he entered into any situation he'd assess it fully and carefully. Once he'd made the decision to go ahead with it, he'd then refuse to worry about it.

How to deal with worry:

i)   Clearly define what you are worrying about. Often, the best way of doing this is by writing it down. Most of time this will make the solution obvious.

ii)   Without going into the realms of fantasy, ask yourself what the realistic worst possible could be. Write it out unequivocally. A lot of worry comes from an unwillingness to face the worst possible situation. Ask yourself the likelihood of this occurring. This process helps to put the problem into context and often helps you realise that it is not as bad as you thought.

iii)   Resolve to accept the worst possible outcome if it occurs. If you accept it fully, then you have no reason to worry.

iv)   Begin immediately doing everything you can to improve upon the worst possible outcome.

        This process transforms a worry into a challenge.

        You can also adapt this process to assess a situation before entering into it.

Anxiety & conscience work
        together to make sure
                one works hard but not
                        often achieves much.

HATRED

"He was angry with me, he attacked me, he defeated me, he robbed me"

- those who dwell on such thoughts will never be free from hatred

- those who do not dwell on such thoughts will surely become free from hatred.

For hatred can never put an end to hatred; love alone can. This is an unalterable law. People forget that their lives will end soon. For those who remember, quarrels come to an end.

The Dharmapada

If somebody does something to upset or hurt you, how should you react? Following the hurt will be anger. Anger leads to thoughts of revenge. But what if you avenge yourself? Will the other person leave it at that? They will also feel hurt and anger and will turn to thoughts of vengeance. If they do take revenge this may well lead to a similar reaction from yourself. Where will it end? When everything you've both worked for is destroyed and one or both of you dead? What will happen then? Will your families carry it on?

And what about nations? If one nation invades, conquers or humiliates another nation, what happens when the slighted nation is in a position to seek vengeance? Where will it end? With genocide?

"An eye for an eye, leaving the whole world blind."

Pain is difficult to take, especially when inflicted by another. But ask yourself this. Have you never done anything to hurt or harm others? Also, who does feelings of anger harm the most? Who gets the most upset and succumbs more to stomach ulcers and high blood pressure? The only path is the path to forgiveness - especially of yourself. It is not an easy route to take and you may need some help. But never be afraid to ask. There are plenty of people in the same boat as you. It's a matter of finding someone you can relate to.

FORGIVENESS

To forgive others will more often free you
more than the ones being forgiven.

He is a man who is impossible to please, because he
is never pleased with himself - Goethe (1747-1832)

Forgive yourself - you are often harsher on
yourself than you are on others, and this is
despite knowing how sorry you are. Remember,
mistakes and failures are life's lessons.

If you go out into the world with an open mind
and try to find the worst person in the world, you
will find that person to be yourself. You will only
see the more glaring of faults in others but if you
look deep inside yourself you will find each of
these faults within yourself, even if only to a tiny
extent. To criticise is easy: the way
forward is to be forgiving of yourself and others.

If someone if constantly late, is it correct to say "They are absolutely hopeless", or "They are a bad timekeeper"? The more judgmental you are, the more angry and frustrated you will become.

It is easy to judge others and be angry towards them when the occasion arises. But how do you know that in the same circumstances and with what they have been through you would not react the same way? The Sioux say: "O Great Spirit, keep me from ever judging and criticising another until I have walked in their moccasins for two weeks."

FEAR

Where fear is, happiness is not -
Seneca (4BC-AD65)

Were the diver
to think on the
jaws of the shark
he would never
lay his hands on
the precious pearl
- Sa'di (1200)

Just as courage imperils life,
fear protects it - Leonardo Da Vinci
(1425-1519)

A good scare is worth more to a man than good advice.
- Edgar Watson Howe (1854-1937)

A man who causes fear cannot be free from fear. - Epicurus (342-270 BC)

Fear produces fatigue. Fatigue prevents us from conquering fear. By breaking this cycle you will release tremendous stores of energy.

Often people fear the worst possible outcome of a situation, even though it is extremely unlikely to occur. Also, if they actually thought the worst possible outcome through, it hardly ever warrants the trepidation they felt about it. Being human is about overcoming groundless fears and anxieties.

LAUGHTER

Laughing and smiling cause chemicals to be released in the brain which produce a kind of euphoria. Also, when laughing stress hormones in the blood - adrenaline and cortisone - are lowered, resulting in one feeling more at peace.

If something upsets you, try to find something funny about it. If one allows oneself to, it is almost always as easy to find something funny about a situation as it is finding something terrible about it.

Pain
is
deeper
than
all
thought;
laughter
is
higher
than
all
pain
- Elbert Hubbard (1859-1915)

No one is more
profoundly sad
than he who laughs
too much
- Jean Paul Richter (1763-1825)

<u>WISDOM</u>

To attain knowledge, add things every day.
To attain wisdom, remove things every
day. - Tao Te Ching

As a flood sweeps away a slumbering
village, death sweeps away those who spend
their lives gathering flowers. Death
sweeps them away whilst they are still
gathering, caught in the pursuit of
pleasure. But the wise live without injuring
nature, as the bee drinks honey without
harming the flower.
- The Dharmapada

Like a lovely flower, full of colour but
lacking in fragrance, are the words of
those who do not practice what they
preach. Like a lovely flower full of colour
and fragrance are the words of those who
practice what they preach.

It is all very well getting what you want out of life: you also need the wisdom to enjoy it once you have it.

What is the point of having all the knowledge in the world, the intellectual ability to demolish anyone in a debate with only a few words and the intelligence to understand and add to any subject area chosen if you don't have the wisdom to live your life in happiness?

To learn from your mistakes is normal. To learn from others' mistakes takes wisdom.

There are those who believe that life should be fair and just and satisfy our needs. Life is not fair and just. Holding this belief will mean that reality will be very painful and we will be constantly disappointed, angry, frustrated and depressed. "Let me have the determination to change what I can change, the serenity to accept what I cannot, and the wisdom to know the difference between the two."

CONTENTMENT

Who is content with nothing possesses all things - Nicolas Boileau (1636-1711)

Do not spoil what you have by desiring what you have not; but remember that what you now have was once among the things only hoped for - Epicurus (342-270 BC)

Better a little fire to warm us than a great one to burn us - Thomas Fuller (1608-1661)

It is the chiefest point of happiness that a man is willing to be what he is
- Desiderius Erasmus (1469-1536)

The secret of happiness is the exploration and enjoyment of genius untainted by your own lack of it
- Baruch Spinoza (1632-1677)

My
crown is
called
content.
A crown
it is
that
seldom
kings
enjoy.
Shake
speare
(1564-
1616)

Everyone is "going-to-be-happy" when they have achieved something or another. When they get there, very few are. The secret is not to have what you want, but to want what you have.

Chinese allegoric tale:

Once there was a stonecutter who was unhappy and wished to be someone else with a different position in life.

One day he passed a wealthy merchant's house and, through an open gateway, saw all of the great possessions the merchant possessed and important visitors. The stonecutter was envious of what he saw and wished he could be exactly like the merchant. Then he would no longer have to be a mere stonecutter.

To his astonishment, his wish was granted and he suddenly became the merchant, and had more power and more luxuries than he ever dreamed of. He was also envied and despised by the poorer people and had more enemies than he had dreamed of.

Then he noticed a high official being transported by servants and surrounded by soldiers. Everyone bowed to the great and mighty official. He was more powerful and more respected than any other throughout the kingdom. "How powerful that official is!" the stonecutter thought, and wished he could be like him.

Again, his wish was granted. But the stonecutter found the official was the most hated and feared man in the kingdom as well, which is why he needed the soldiers to guard him, and the heat of the sun made the official very uncomfortable and weary in his heavy robes. He looked up at the fierce sun shining brightly in the sky and said: "How powerful it is, I wish I could be the sun."

No sooner had he wished it than he became the sun, shining down on earth. But a big black cloud came along and blocked the sun's rays. "How mighty the cloud is," he thought "I wish I was as powerful as the cloud."

Then he became the cloud covering the sun's rays and raining down on the villages. But a mighty wind came and blew the cloud away. "I wish I could be as powerful as the wind" - as soon as he thought this, he became the wind.

But whilst the wind could uproot trees and destroy whole villages, it soon came across a great boulder. The huge stone was immovable, resisting the wind.

Sure enough, he wished to be the boulder, and he became it. He was now happy at last - the most powerful force of everything on earth. But then he heard a noise. Chink. Chink. Chink. Chink. Chink. A hammer was banging a chisel into the stone, breaking it away, piece by piece. "What could be more powerful than I?" he thought, and there at the foot of the great stone was... a stonecutter.

OPTIMISM VERSUS PESSIMISM

An adventure is an inconvenience rightly viewed. An inconvenience is an adventure wrongly viewed.

It is better to be an optimist and have everything go wrong, than a pessimist and have everything go right.

Optimist: "My glass is half full"
Pessimist: "My glass is half empty"

Who is more likely to get out of bed in the morning eager to face the day: the person who expects the worst from the day, or the person who anticipates a fantastic day? There is no point in building castles in the air, but there is almost always two ways to look at everything - with pessimism and foreboding or with optimism and expectation.

Those who are down on life seldom accomplish anything much. They look at situations with pessimism. They never think clearly or objectively at things, and they don't recognise or believe in their own abilities - the same abilities which are blindingly obvious to many of those around them. It is out of the question that they stretch these abilities to overcome even the smallest amount of risk, unlike their optimistic but less talented counterparts who enjoy life and accomplish much more.

GIVING

Recall the face of the poorest and most helpless person whom you may have seen and ask yourself if the next step you contemplate is going to be of any use to him, will he gain anything from it? Will it restore him to control over his life and destiny? In other words, will it lead to swaraj, self-rule, for the hungry and also the spiritually starved millions of countrymen? Then you will find your doubts and your self melting away. - Gandhiji's Talisman (1869-1948)

Many people think that by acquiring more money and owning more things they will be happy. But it is often by giving that greater happiness is found.

Happiness - the more you give the more you get back.

Only the meanest of people will resent your good fortune if you share it.

POSITIVE MENTAL ATTITUDE

Thoughts are causes: conditions are effects. Any feelings we have are preceded by a thought which causes that feeling. The same is true about where we are in life - in order to change the direction of your life the most fundamental change you often have to make is in that of your thinking.

Positive people have been positive and optimistic for so long that, like the committed pessimist, it has become a habit, something natural that they do unquestioningly. If you are down on life, when you next feel yourself thinking about a bad memory, replace it with a good memory. When you next ponder needlessly over the worst possible outcome of a situation, bring to mind a possible positive one. You will be surprised how quickly you can change your habits by determined effort.

Be careful what you think, for what you think most of the time will determine how much inner peace you have.

If you think constantly of the injustices you have undergone, the times people have been rude and nasty to you and how the world is a cruel place you will become cynical and full of resentment. You will wear a frown. People will not want to know you, which will compound your view of the world.

On the other hand, if you think largely of when people have been kind and fair to you and how the world can be a good place to be you will find life to be far more agreeable. You will find yourself smiling more. People will smile back and be more pleasant.

This is how to change a negative attitude: whenever you find yourself thinking bitter thoughts, replace them with memories of pleasant times and when people have been good and fair. If you find it difficult to do this, write down times when you have felt happy and people have been good to you whenever you feel at enough peace to do so. Keep adding to this list whenever you can - you will find that it is soon very long. Then, whenever you find yourself entering negative thoughts, read that list and remind yourself life can be good.

When you feel down
you will inevitably
focus on what
you haven't got
but this is exactly
the time you should take account
of what
you have got.

When advanced in years,
you will inevitably
think back to times past.
If you recall only the
times of satisfaction and enjoyment,
excluding all the unpleasant times,
you will find that you are very young,
if not in infancy.

It is very difficult to stop thoughts entering your mind. It is also very difficult to hold two thoughts in your mind simultaneously. It is up to you whether hold a positive or negative thought in your mind.

"Birds of a feather flock together." If you continually and exclusively associate with negative, pessimistic, cynical non-hopers you will become the same yourself. The opposite is also true: a positive environment and positive friends and colleagues are vital if you want to be positive yourself.

<u>IMPORTANCE OF GOALS</u>

Happiness
does
not
lie
in
happiness,
but
in
the
achievement
of
it
- Dostoevsky
(1821-1881)

If
you
are
not
careful,
life
is
what
happens
to
you
whilst
you
are
thinking
about
what
to
do
with
it.

There are those who believe that there are lots of interesting things out there to entertain and keep us all happy. However, if we just sit back and expect to be entertained we will end up bored and unsatisfied. Real satisfaction, in the long term, comes from active participation and skill development rather than passive receiving. Getting actively involved and committed means taking risks, facing new experiences, and facing fears. What you get out is proportional to what you put in.

In 1953 the whole of the graduating year at Harvard University were asked if they had any specific goals or ambitions. Less than 3% had. That year's graduates' careers were followed over the next 25 years. It was found that the 3% who had goals had more stable marriages, better health and were financially worth more than the other 97% put together. They led far, far happier lives.

The most basic requirement in life is the need for purpose, and that is what goals give us. Without goals we drift aimlessly. However, if we have something to aim for the stresses and strains of life are put into context - they become no more than obstacles to overcome to reach the goal. Goals can even make pain more bearable (for example, POWs in WW2 Japanese camps with goals survived longer than the ones who didn't). Goals make the hard times easier, and the good times better.

Happiness is more often created than found.

Goals focus the mind on pleasure: lack of goals focuses the mind on avoiding pain.

Change is inevitable in our society. Goals enable us to control the direction of change in our lives, so that it leads to improvement and not deterioration. It is impossible to control your life without goals.

There are many who would never dream of taking their own lives, but sit back and watch their lives pass them by moment after moment, day after day, month after month, year after year without making any effort to be happy. What is the difference?

Goals are important in life. They give you a focus and a purpose. They give you something to work for, something on which to concentrate your energies. They stop you floundering and falling into an abyss of inertia and depression.

However, the end goal should not become an obsession. One should not sacrifice too much for its achievement for, often, its achievement does not bring the happiness and fulfilment one dreamed of.

Instead, the goal should be looked on as a path to follow. When following this path you should look around you, enjoy each task for what it is and notice how you are developing and learning. This is often the most valuable part of the journey, the part which people all too frequently become too obsessed to notice.

GOAL SETTING & ACHIEVING

Imagine you have lived your life and are thinking back over it. From what type of surroundings would you like to be having those memories? Which part of the world would you like to be in and what type of dwelling would you like to be living in? When thinking over the past from that dwelling, which memories would give you the greatest satisfaction? What would you have liked to have spent your life doing? Where would you like to have visited? Who and what type of people would you have liked to have known? What type of person would have liked to have become?

This exercise will help you to realise what you want out of life.

However, you may find at some point that you no longer want what you once wanted. If you find this is the case, the time has come to review your goals by redoing the exercise.

Very few people achieve much in life because very few know what they really want. This is because their parents, their peers, the media, their teachers are all telling them what they should want. We are told to be happy we must have lots of money, a big house, the latest TV, a flash car, lots of friends, a partner, children, respect... But where do your real values lie? Is it good health, spirituality, family, helping others, material success...? It is not until you decide what you, in your heart of hearts, really want that you will have the commitment to truly strive for it. Have 3 to 5 basic values and prioritise them. You can do this by looking at what you do under pressure: when forced to choose to go one way or another, you always go in the direction that is consistent with your dominant value at the time. Being aware of your values will allow you to set specific goals.

Review your values twice a year for you, like a beautiful flower, are subtly changing all the time.

A useful exercise do to when setting goals (write down the answers):

i)   What are the 3-5 basic values in life that are the most important to you?

ii)   In 30 seconds or less, write down the 3 most important goals in your life right now.

iii)   What would you do if you won £1,000,000 tomorrow? In other words, if you had all the time and money what is the first thing you'd do? And the second?

iv)   How would you spend your time if you only had 6 months to live? (You would be in perfect health until then.)

v)   What have you always wanted to do but have been afraid to attempt?

vi)   Looking back at everything you've

done in life, doing what sort of things in what sort of circumstances gives you the greatest feeling of importance and satisfaction?

vii) If you received one wish, what would it be? This is really your great ambition or dream in life.

After answering these questions it is essential to pick one definite purpose at a time. If you try to achieve several things at once, you diffuse your effort and achieve almost nothing. Also, the accomplishment of that one thing will lead to the attainment of many of the minor things in life.

Why goals should be written down and made specific:

i)   Writing down a goal makes it visible, obvious, concrete and specific.

ii)   Writing a goal down entails a commitment. If you don't write it down, you can always say to yourself, "I never really meant to do that anyway," and leave your options open. Writing goals down challenges procrastination.

Goals cannot be contradictory - for example, you cannot want to spend half your time on the beach and also become an expert government advisor on climate change - either drop one or modify both.
Goals have to be congruent with your fundamental values.
Goals should not be unattainable - eg "I want to be world tennis champion by next summer" should be modified to "I want to win 90% of my club tournament matches next summer."

Potentially useful questions to ask when working towards a goal:

- Why am I not reaching this goal?
- What is standing in my way?
- How can I proceed now?
- How far have I come already?
- How much further do I need to go?
- Am I being realistic?
- Am I being too perfect?

Often, when one opportunity passes by unseized, we will spend so much time and energy regretting our mistake that we will not even notice when another opportunity arises.

ACHIEVEMENT & PERSISTENCE

If one door closes, it is up to you to open another.

Three stages to success:
- Decide what you want out of life
- Find out what you need to do in order to achieve it
- Resolve to do what is needed

    Very few people achieve success because they fall down at one of these stages.

You must lose a fly to catch a trout - George Herbert (1593-1633)

How to manage time effectively:

- Have clear, specific, measurable goals.
- Have clear, detailed plans to achieve those goals.
- Month by month, week by week, day by day, make a list of the things you have to.
- Prioritise the items on the list and number them.
- Do not do anything which is not on the list - put anything new that comes up on the list and renumber the list so that the new item is in the correct priority. When on the list, it does not seem as urgent or important as when reacting to it.
- Concentrate on one thing at a time and do it until it is finished. Then move on to the next in your numbered sequence.
- Lists make you more organised, stop you forgetting to do things, stop you panicking lest you forget and give you a sense of accomplishment when you see a list at the end of the day with the tasks ticked off.

Compared to what we ought to be, we're only half awake. Our fires are damp, our drafts are checked. We make use of only a small part of our mental and physical resources... The human individual thus lives far within his limits. He possesses powers of various sorts which he habitually fails to use. He energises below his maximum and he behaves below his optimum.
- William Jones (1746-1794)

Nothing in the world can take the place of persistence. Talent will not; nothing is more common than unsuccessful men with talent. Genius will not; unrewarded genius is almost a proverb. Education alone will not; the world is full of educated derelicts. Persistence and determination are omnipotent.
- Calvin Coolidge (1872-1933)

Agree with the omnipotence of
achievement & persistence? Read on...

Apparently, Colonel Sanders recipe
was rejected over 1000 times before
finally being taken up. What does
this tell us? That if you don't give
up, you <u>will</u> succeed? Or does it tell
us that you need a certain type of
personality to succeed in such
adverse conditions? Some people
thrive on this type of challenge, but
most enter mental illness, often
resulting in a nervous breakdown.
Yes, we hear about persistence
succeeding but is this because it is so
rare it is newsworthy? Why do you
never hear about persistence failing?
It is because persistence doesn't

fail or is it because it isn't newsworthy? Ask yourself what would happen if your ideas were rejected even 100 times. Would you carry on or would you be despairing? Try it to see. If it is patently obvious that this type of challenge is not congruous with your personality, divert your energies into finding what will make you happy, but without such tremendous effort (you may find you enjoy simple pleasures like eating well, keeping fit, reading good books, watching funny films or whatever <u>you</u> like). Life can be enjoyable without being a struggle: success isn't everything. Remember that persistence isn't necessarily healthy: stalking is a form of persistence.

In our society those who make vast fortunes, strive for great causes, make important scientific break-throughs, show amazing courage are looked up to and used as role models. However, those who are simply happy in everyday, mundane life are thought of as irrelevant.

Happy the man
                    who learns
            early the wide
                        chasm that
lies
between his
                            wishes
                and
his powers!
-

Johann W von Goethe (1749-
1832)

<u>PHYSICAL</u>

A well person wears a crown which only an ill person can see – Egyptian proverb

The physical results of a sedentary life, amongst other things, is muscular atrophy, physical weakness, calcium loss from bones.

People who do not exercise regularly are also more prone to tension, depression, anxiety and mental fatigue. Part of the reason for this is that exercise causes the brain to release hormones called endorphins. These are natural stimulants, which are released in greater quantities if the exercise is aerobic - ie any activity or sport in which you breath as you exercise - eg brisk walking, cycling, swimming. 30 minutes aerobic exercise everyday are the current recommended levels.

Who has more,
a terminally ill
rich person
whose illness
is causing
them to be
bedridden and
in immense
physical and
mental pain, or
a penniless
healthy
person?

<u>DESIDERATA</u>

Go placidly amid the noise and haste,
and remember what peace there may
be in silence.

As far as possible be on
good terms with all persons.

Speak your truth quietly and clearly and
listen to others, even the dull and
ignorant; they too have their own story.

Avoid loud and aggressive persons:
they are vexations to the spirit.

If you compare yourself with others
you may become vain and bitter, for
there will always be greater and
lesser persons than yourself.

Enjoy your achievements as well as
your plans. Keep interested in your
career however humble; it is a
possession in the changing fortunes
of time.

Exercise caution in your business
affairs; the world is full of trickery.

But let this not blind you to what
virtue there is. Many persons strive
for high ideals and everywhere
life is full of heroism.

Be yourself.

Especially do not feign affection.

Neither be cynical about love, for in
the face of all aridity and disenchantment,
it is as perennial as the grass.

Take kindly to the counsel of the
years, gracefully surrendering the
things of youth.

Nurture strength of spirit to shield
you in sudden misfortune. But do
not distress yourself with imaginings.

Many fears are born of fatigue
and loneliness.

Beyond a wholesome discipline, be
gentle with yourself. You are a child
of the universe, no less than the
trees and the stars.

You have a right to be here. And
whether or not it is clear to you,
no doubt the universe is unfolding
as it should.

Therefore be at peace with God,
whatever you conceive Him to be and
whatever your labours and aspirations
in the noisy confusion of life, keep
peace with your soul.

With all its sham and drudgery and
broken dreams, it is still a beautiful world.

Be careful.

Strive to be happy

- Found in Old St Pauls Church, Baltimore,
dated 1692

... AND FINALLY

There are many paths to happiness - don't die choosing!

This page is here 'cos a book looks incomplete without a blank page at the back of it